C000130464

Delicious

Anti – Inflammatory Diet

Smoothie Recipes

Plant Based Ingredients

Melody Rayne

Table of Contents

If you are wanting to live a healthy, anti – inflammatory lifestyle, these delicious smoothie recipes will make a great addition to your everyday diet! These are some of my personal favorite smoothie recipes that I rotate in my diet weekly. Give them a taste! They are anti – inflammatory, and the ingredients are whole foods.

Enjoy!

Green Coconut & Guava

Ingredients:

- 1 guava, sliced
- 1 large avocado
- 12/4 cup coconut milk
- 1 lemon juice
- 4 ice cubes

Directions:

1. Add all ingredients into the blender as you desire and blend until smooth.

2. Serve immediately and enjoy!

Nutritional Value (Amount per Serving):

- Calories 512
- Fat 18 g
- Carbohydrates 74 g
- Protein 6 g

CREAMY AVOCADO

Ingredients:

- 1 cup cranberries
- 1 banana (frozen if possible)
- 1 avocado
- 1 cup almond milk, unsweetened
- 6 ice cubes

Directions:

1. Add all ingredients into the blender and blend until smooth and creamy.

2. Serve & enjoy!

Nutritional Value (Amount per Serving):

- Calories 432
- Fat 16 g
- Carbohydrates 75 g
- Protein 6 g

Avocado Apricot Smoothie

Ingredients:

- 6 apricots, pitted
- 1 large avocado
- 1 cup coconut water or milk
- 1 cup blue berries frozen
- 2 mint leaves
- 2 - 4 ice cubes

Directions:

1. Add all ingredients into the blender and blend until smooth and creamy.
2. Serve immediately and enjoy!

Nutritional Value (Amount per Serving):

- Calories 575
- Fat 16 g
- Carbohydrates 77 g
- Protein 7 g

Notes: Variations: Schedule: Other:

BLUEBERRY AVOCADO SMOOTHIE

Ingredients:

- 1/2 cup blueberries
- 1 avocado
- 1/2 cup water
- 1 cup baby spinach
- 1 lime juice
- 4 – 8 ice cubes

Directions:

1. Add all ingredients into the blender and blend until smooth.

2. Serve & enjoy!

Nutritional Value (Amount per Serving):

- Calories 483
- Fat 16 g
- Carbohydrates 76 g
- Protein 7 g

Notes: Variations: Schedule: Other:

HONEYDEW FIG SMOOTHIE

Ingredients:

- 1 cup honeydew melon
- 1 inch ginger
- 4 figs
- 1 ripe banana
- 1 cup vanilla almond milk
- 4 ice cubes

Directions:

1. Add all ingredients into the blender and blend until smooth.
2. Serve & enjoy!

Nutritional Value (Amount per Serving):

- Calories 328
- Fat 2 g
- Carbohydrates 80 g
- Protein 2 g

Coconut Fig Smoothie

Ingredients:

- 1 guava, sliced
- 4 tbsp coconut milk
- 2 – 4 figs
- 1 cup fresh raspberries
- 1 lime juice
- 4 ice cubes

Directions:

3. Add all ingredients into the blender and blend until smooth.
4. Serve immediately and enjoy!

Nutritional Value (Amount per Serving):

- Calories 412
- Fat 8 g
- Carbohydrates 74 g
- Protein 2 g

CREAMY FIG SMOOTHIE

Ingredients:

- 1 cup cranberries

- 1 banana (frozen if possible)

- 4 figs

- 1 cup almond milk, unsweetened

- 6 ice cubes

Directions:

3. Add all ingredients into the blender and blend until smooth and creamy.

4. Serve & enjoy!

Nutritional Value (Amount per Serving):

- Calories 332

- Fat 2 g

- Carbohydrates 75 g

- Protein 2 g

Minty Apricot Smoothie

Ingredients:

- 4 apricots, pitted
- 4 figs
- 1 cup coconut water
- 1 cup mix berries frozen
- 2 mint leaves
- 2 - 4 ice cubes

Directions:

3. Add all ingredients into the blender and blend until smooth and creamy.

4. Serve immediately and enjoy!

Nutritional Value (Amount per Serving):

- Calories 375
- Fat 1 g
- Carbohydrates 77 g
- Protein 2 g

Blueberry Pear Smoothie

Ingredients:

- 1/2 cup blueberries
- 2 – 4 figs
- 1/2 cup water
- 1 pear, seeded and diced
- 1 lemon juice
- 4 – 8 ice cubes

Directions:

3. Add all ingredients into the blender and blend until smooth.

4. Serve & enjoy!

Nutritional Value (Amount per Serving):

- Calories 283
- Fat 1 g
- Carbohydrates 66 g
- Protein 2 g

Green Mango Smoothie

Ingredients

- ½ cup frozen blueberries
- 1 cup frozen mango chunks
- 1 cup original almond milk, unsweetened
- 1 squeezed lemon juice
- 1 tbsp. raw coconut butter*
- 2 cups baby spinach
- 4-6 ice cubes

Substitute with almond butter, if desired.

Directions

1. Combine ingredients in a blender. Cover and blend until smooth.

2. Serve & enjoy!

Nutritional Information (per serving)

- Calories 275
- Fat 7 g
- Carbohydrates 44 g
- Protein 2 g

MINTY GREEN BERRY

Ingredients

- ¾ cup broccoli florets, de-stemmed
- 1 cups coconut water
- 1 cup blueberries
- 1 orange, peeled and separated
- 1/2 cup orange juice - optional
- 4 mint leaves
- 3-4 ice cubes

Directions

1. In a medium sauce pan, bring water to a boil. Boil broccoli for 7 minutes, or until tender. Or use flash frozen.

2. Combine ingredients in a blender. Cover and blend until smooth.

3. Serve & enjoy!

Nutritional Information (per serving)

- Calories 175
- Fat 1`g
- Carbohydrates 39 g
- Protein 3 g

CREAMY KALE & BLACKBERRY SMOOTHIE

Ingredients

- 1 ½ cups blackberries
- ½ cup original almond milk, unsweetened
- 2 tbsp. creamy almond butter
- 1 tsp. cinnamon
- 1 tsp. vanilla extract
- 1 cup green kale
- 4-6 ice cubes
- Optional: add 1 Tbsp. raw honey

Directions

1. Combine ingredients in a blender. Cover and blend until smooth.
2. Serve &enjoy!

Nutritional Information (per serving)

- Calories 266
- Fat 12 g
- Carbohydrates 40 g
- Protein 4 g

BABY GREEN SMOOTHIE

Ingredients

- 2 cups baby spinach
- 2 celery stalks, chopped
- 1 kiwi, peeled
- 3 mint leaves
- 1 cup apple juice
- 4-6 ice cubes

Directions

1. Combine ingredients in a blender. Cover and blend until smooth.
2. Serve & enjoy!

Nutritional Information (per serving)

- Calories 164
- Fat 0 g
- Carbohydrates 40g
- Protein 1 g

BANANA PEANUT BUTTER SMOOTHIE

Ingredients

- 1 large banana, peeled
- 2 tbsp. creamy peanut butter
- 2 cups baby spinach
- ½ low-fat yogurt, plain
- ½ cup original almond milk, unsweetened
- 4-6 ice cubes

Directions

1. Combine ingredients in a blender. Cover and blend until smooth.

2. Serve & enjoy!

Nutritional Information (per serving)

- Calories 372
- Fat 12 g
- Carbohydrates 40 g
- Protein 6 g

Your reviews are thanked in advance!

If you are looking for some really fun blank recipe books to either write your own recipes, or give as gifts, check these books out on Amazon! People love using them to keep all of their best recipes inside one place! They make great gifts as well! We have hundreds of styles! Look them up under Recipe Junkies blank recipes, cookbooks.

Blank Cookbook

Recipe Journal

Blank
Cookbook

My Recipe Journal

Blank Cookbook

My
Recipes

Blank Cookbook

Blank cookbook

Recipe Journal

Dads Recipe Log

Blank Cookbook

Vegan
Recipe Journal

My Favorite Vegan Recipes

Disclaimer: All rights reserved. No part of this book may be reproduced or transmitted in any form or by any means, electronic or mechanical, including photocopying, recording or by any information storage and retrieval system, without written permission from the author, except for the inclusion of brief quotations in a review. The information provided in this book is designed to provide helpful information on the subjects discussed. This book is not meant to be used, nor should it be used, to diagnose or treat any medical condition. For diagnosis or treatment of any medical problem, consult your own physician. The publisher and author are not responsible for any specific health or allergy needs that may require medical supervision and are not liable for any damages or negative consequences from any treatment, action, application or preparation, to any person reading or following the information in this book. References are provided for informational purposes only and do not constitute endorsement of any websites or other sources. Readers should be aware that the websites listed in this book may change.

Printed in Great Britain
by Amazon

32732267R00030